JULIUS CAESAR

Leaders of the Ancient World

JULIUS CAESAR

Margaux Baum and
James Thorne

ROSEN
PUBLISHING

New York

Published in 2017 by The Rosen Publishing Group, Inc.
29 East 21st Street, New York, NY 10010

First Edition

Library of Congress Cataloging-in-Publication Data

Names: Baum, Margaux, author. | Thorne, James, 1974– author.
Title: Julius Caesar / Margaux Baum and James Thorne.
Description: First edition. | New York City : The Rosen Publishing Group, Inc., 2017. | Series: Leaders of the ancient world | Includes bibliographical references and index. | Audience: Grades 7–12.
Identifiers: LCCN 2016030402 | ISBN 9781508172482 (library bound)
Subjects: LCSH: Caesar, Julius—Juvenile literature. | Heads of state—Rome—Biography—Juvenile literature. | Generals—Rome—Biography—Juvenile literature. | Rome—History—Republic, 265–30 B.C.—Juvenile literature.
Classification: LCC DG261 .T53 2017 | DDC 973/.05092 [B]—dc23
LC record available at https://lccn.loc.gov/2016030402

Manufactured in Malaysia

CONTENTS

INTRODUCTION

The conquest of new lands by powerful and charismatic leaders has occurred time and again throughout history. However, few ancient empires we study nowadays had the longevity, stability, strength, and influence of the Roman Empire. At the turn of the first millennium, around the lifetime of Jesus Christ, the extent of Rome's possessions in and adjoining Europe was vast. More than thirty nations now exist in what was then the Roman Empire. Most of Europe, North Africa, and large parts of the Middle East were united under Roman rule. This included a common monetary currency, the legal system, and Rome's official language, Latin, which was used widely in its dominion.

The time of prolonged political chaos that ushered in the Roman Empire nearly wiped out what the Romans had built over the previous few centuries, under the Roman Republic. Even as the Romans conquered their formerly more powerful neighbors—including the Athenian and Spartan Greeks and the Macedonians, once led by Alexander the Great—tensions within Rome itself threatened to tear it, and its empire, apart.

This bronze bust of Julius Caesar, one of many representations of the famous Roman leader, is found in the Vatican Museum, in Vatican City, Italy.

Civil strife in 133 BCE sparked when Tiberius Gracchus, a reformer, perished with hundreds of his supporters in Rome itself, fighting his own countrymen. Gaius Gracchus, his brother, suffered the same fate a little over a decade later, in 121 BCE. Not long after Julius Caesar was born in 100 BCE, Rome's authority was challenged by its own generals marching on the city in separate incidents. One of these even included Caesar's own uncle, Gaius Marius.

Rome had arisen as a collection of villages alongside the Tiber River around 900 BCE. By about 600 BCE, it was a prosperous city-state, and by 300 BCE it had cemented its control over the entire Italian peninsula. Its strength, influence, and territory seemed to increase exponentially over the ensuing two centuries. The innovative and almost revolutionary government it had set up—a republic with greater freedoms and representation, influenced by Greek democracy—suffered growing pains as Rome grew. A system that worked efficiently and responded to the needs of many of its people when Rome was a smaller state began to suffer the bigger Rome's empire grew. Dissatisfaction grew with the wealthier Romans who had monopolized power.

One man, however, forced political change with the force of his will and sought to rule by himself rather than deal with the power struggles and intrigue of his countrymen. The man who brought dictatorship back to Rome, Julius Caesar, rose to win the hearts of Rome's masses. He was a statesman and also a scholar and writer, but he is particularly well known for being one of the most brilliant military leaders in history.

While it was Augustus, his nephew, who would later solidify Rome's transformation from republic to empire, ushering in an even more powerful era for the nation and its conquests, it was Caesar who lit the spark and stoked the fire. He laid the foundations for Rome to reach its greatest size and influence.

CHAPTER 1

CAESAR'S EARLY YEARS

In 100 BCE, Gaius Julius Caesar was born to a patrician (upper-class) family known as the gens Julia, in Rome. His extended family claimed to have been descended from Iulus. Iulus was supposedly the son of the mythological Trojan prince Aeneas and also a descendent of the mythic founders of Rome, Romulus and Remus. They themselves were considered children of the Roman goddess Venus. From the very beginning, a man of Caesar's heritage could expect to enter a career in public life, beginning with training for military service. He would go abroad to serve in the Roman legions around the age of twenty and later work to be a member of the Senate by about age thirty. A life in politics was his likely eventual destination, perhaps with employment in the law courts as an advocate (lawyer) or judge in the interim. Those who worked hard and exhibited talent could expect appointment to very high public offices. Exceptional leaders would go on to be generals or the governors of Roman provinces.

Rome did not have a huge government like a modern state, with many departments and civil servants. Instead, a number of magistrates were appointed each year. These men governed the city and the provinces with the help of small staffs of their friends and slaves. The different magistrates had very specific roles, and there was a strict progression upward from junior posts to senior posts. The progression was known as the *cursus honorum*, and it ran from quaestor (twenty were appointed each year), to praetor (eight each year), to consul. There was also an optional rank of *curule aedile* (two were appointed each year), and every fifth year two censors—very senior men, who had to have been consuls—were appointed. In addition to these offices, there was an important emergency post, that of dictator. In a supreme crisis, a dictator could be appointed. He would be given supreme power, even outranking the consuls, for six months. The office was viewed with some suspicion, as it gave more or less kingly authority to whoever held the post, and it was very seldom used.

AN ARISTOCRAT'S EDUCATION

The Roman aristocracy expected its boys to follow the senatorial career, and their education prepared them accordingly. Young Caesar would have learned Greek. This was essential for all cultured Romans, as it was the language of many of the arts and sciences, and it was more widely spoken than Latin throughout the Mediterranean. His historical studies would have included the campaigns of Alexander the Great, a figure who clearly remained fixed in Caesar's imagination for the rest of his life. Although he died young, Alexander had conquered vast areas of Asia in a whirlwind career of just ten years. Roman boys destined for a political career also, very naturally, studied rhetoric, the skill of speaking persuasively to an audience.

In the earliest stories we know about Caesar, he shows the traits of his character that later became well known. As a young soldier, in the assault on Mytilene, the chief city of the Greek island of Lesbos, he showed his bravery. The eighteen-year-old legionary won the civic crown, an award given for saving a fellow soldier's life in battle. Another story, which comes from his trip to the island of Rhodes to continue his rhetorical studies at the age of twenty- four, shows that his charm, commanding presence, and ruthlessness were already well formed. On the trip, Caesar was captured by pirates. Many bands of pirates plagued the Mediterranean at that time. They demanded a ransom of twenty talents of silver to set him free. A talent was a weight of about 30 kilograms (66 pounds).

Caesar laughed and astonished the outlaws by saying he was worth fifty talents. He sent his companions to collect the money. During six weeks in captivity, he joined in the pirates' games, called them illiterate barbarians, and ordered them to be quiet whenever he wanted to sleep. He also promised them that once they set him free, he would have them crucified—the normal punishment for piracy. He kept his word, too. Once released, he hired several galleys, hunted down the pirates, and executed them. They were crucified, but to spare them a long, agonizing death, Caesar ordered their throats to be cut as they were nailed up.

MILITARY REFORMS

Ancient city-states were often at war, but they hardly ever maintained standing armies as we know them today. Instead, when needed, most citizens were expected to serve, except the poorest, who could not afford their own weapons (the state did not provide these). Slaves, of course, were not trusted to bear arms.

Most people lived on the land as farmers, and the campaigning season did not start until after the harvest in August. Soldiers worried about their farms and were anxious to get home after a few months in time to plant the next year's crops. But there was an important political advantage in this system of citizen-soldiers. Military service for all meant defense of the people, by the people.

As Rome extended its power, campaigns were conducted at greater distances from the city and lasted for more than one season. Soldiers were called upon to stay overseas or along distant frontiers over winter, and so military service became increasingly unpopular among farmers. Instead, the landless poor started to fill the ranks of the legions. These people saw soldiering as a profitable profession, and far from wanting discharge, they wanted to work for as long as possible.

In 107 BCE, consul Gaius Marius, who was Caesar's uncle, was put in command of the unpopular war in Numidia, already in its fifth year. For the first time in Rome's history, he took an army of landless volunteers. There were military advantages in this new system but also political dangers. The volunteers served for plunder, and so the more successful a general was, the more loyal they were to him and the less loyal they were to the community as a whole.

A TIME OF TROUBLES

The first two decades of Caesar's life were troubled times in Italy, and as he grew up he must have watched developments with interest. Two major wars rocked Italy at this time: the Social War (91–89 BCE) and the First Civil War (84–82 BCE) fought between the supporters of Caesar's uncle, Gaius Marius, and those of Marius's rival, Sulla. At the same time, Mithradates VI, a Greek king, took advantage of the Romans' problems at home to overrun their territory in Asia Minor (modern Turkey).

The Glypothek museum in Munich, Germany, houses this bust of Roman dictator Sulla, which hails from the first century BCE.

The Social War was fought between Rome and its Italian allies (*socius* is Latin for "ally") for the following reason. Long before, Italy had contained many independent city-states that had constantly warred with each other. By the first century BCE, Rome had come out of these conflicts as the most powerful city and had imposed peace. Under Rome's treaties with these allied city-states, each city-state had to provide a certain number of troops for the Roman army. In this way, the city-states made a large contribution to Roman power. But because their people did not have Roman citizenship, they could not vote and had no influence on how this increased power was used. They resented this taxation (in manpower) without representation, but instead of fighting a war of independence, they wanted their cities to become formally part of the Roman state. Then they themselves would become full citizens on equal terms.

The war was sparked when the leaders of their movement were murdered, after which most of the Italians revolted. Although the Romans sent armies against the Italian cities, by 90 BCE the situation was so out of their control that the Italian cities gave in to the Romans' demands. At first, the Romans gave full citizenship to the communities that had stayed loyal. Later, they had to promise it even to the rebellious cities in return for peace. All Italians south of the Po River were now Roman citizens in a unified territory.

THE FIRST CIVIL WAR

The mopping up after the Social War took some years, and before it was really over, the First Civil War, the struggle between Marius and Sulla, began. Marius (born around 157 BCE) was one of Rome's greatest soldiers. He had reformed the army, turning it from a part-time militia into an effective professional fighting force. He had put an end to a troublesome war in Numidia in North Africa in 105 BCE, and then in two battles in 102 and 101 BCE, he destroyed a horde of Celtic and Germanic tribes who were invading northern Italy over the Alps. During this period, he was elected consul six times. He was a poor politician, however.

Lucius Cornelius Sulla, born around 138 BCE, had been Marius's quaestor (second in command) in Numidia. There, his daring and skillful diplomacy contributed greatly to the Roman victory.

This painting by John Vanderlyn, *Gaius Marius Amid the Ruins of Carthage* (1807), portrays Marius in the ruins of the city after the Romans destroyed it.

Both men fought for the Roman side in the Social War, but once it was over, they quarreled over who was to command the war against Mithradates VI in Asia.

Mithradates's kingdom, Pontus, was rich, since it was blessed with fertile fields and numerous mines from which salt as well as precious metals were extracted. It was expected that whoever went as the Roman general would reap a colossal harvest of plunder. The people elected Sulla as one of the consuls for 88 BCE, and the Senate voted to put him in command of the campaign against Mithradates.

But Marius would not yield. He had a law proposed that would transfer back to him both Sulla's command and the army he had raised. Although Marius won the vote, the changes he had made to the army now backfired on him. Sulla refused to give up his army. Worse, the soldiers he had recruited stayed loyal to him in defiance of the law. The stage had been reached where Roman troops could choose to obey their general rather than the Senate and the people.

Over the next fifty years, such occasions, where ambitious men claimed the loyalties of

The Roman legionnaire, memorialized by this statue, was one of the best trained and most effective soldiers in the history of warfare and key to Rome's imperial expansion.

their soldiers against the state, would become more and more frequent. Sulla immediately marched on Rome. He was the first of Rome's generals to do this, but not the last. It was the year that Caesar had his twelfth birthday. He was growing up in a world where previously unthinkable things were becoming possible. Forty years later, he would march on the capital, too.

For now, Marius was totally unprepared and fled to Africa, while Sulla took control of the city and overturned Marius's laws. Sulla then departed for Greece to take over the war against Mithradates. Marius's next move, although he was now seventy years of age, was to collect an army of veterans of his old campaigns and make his own march on Rome.

When occupying the city, Marius let loose his men for five days and nights of slaughter. Sulla was outlawed. Once order was restored, Marius proclaimed himself and his ally, Cinna, consuls for 86 BCE. This was his last act. A few days into the new year he died, leaving his faction with no leader that could compare to him. Cinna ruled alone until Sulla returned.

SULLA OCCUPIES ROME

Sulla defeated Mithradates in 84 BCE and returned to invade Italy. Many young nobles, including Marcus Crassus and the as-yet unheard-of Pompey, joined him. Sulla occupied Rome with ease. He had himself made dictator and set about exterminating Marius's supporters. The so-called proscriptions, the lists of enemies to be killed, reduced the Senate to far below its traditional three hundred members, but Sulla brought it up to a strength of six hundred by packing it with his own supporters. The property of Sulla's victims included ten thousand slaves. These he confiscated, and later, by granting them their freedom, he made them into a large and loyal force of street fighters to add to his army.

But although Sulla was ferocious and ruthless, he also used his power for the public good. He did restore peace, and when he had done this, he retired, as he had promised. On laying down the office of dictator in the Forum, he became a private citizen again, and although he had surely made many deadly enemies, he walked alone back to his house, quite unprotected.

A FRAGILE REPUBLIC

In the half-mythical past, the Romans had been ruled by kings. In Caesar's time, these kings were remembered as being cruel and proud. The last, Tarquinius Superbus, was reportedly so unpopular that in 510 BCE he was expelled from Rome. After that, the Romans had a fear of one-man rule. The constitution they devised after the kings supposedly instituted government for the people by the people. Rome thus became a republic (*res publica* is Latin for "the public affair"). The constitution distributed power to several bodies, which, in theory at least, were meant to balance each other. This was so no one body would gain absolute power.

The sovereign body was the *comitia*, the assembly of all the common people. Only the comitia could pass laws. It also elected the magistrates. In principle, this was democratic, but flawed. There was no mechanism for proper debate, so in effect the people had only a yes/no choice on whatever motions were proposed. Also, the voting procedure favored certain groups. Voting was done by large groups of people known as centuries, and the rich controlled more centuries than the common people.

The Senate was composed of those ex-magistrates who had held the rank of curule aedile or above. It controlled foreign affairs and finance. Significantly, it was small enough to allow proper debate, and it included many experienced men. To protect the people, a group of magistrates called

A Roman senator speaks to his assembled colleagues in a temple. The Senate, ideally, served as a check on monarchs or other leaders seeking too much power.

the tribunes of the people sat in on meetings. They had the power to veto or block any motion.

The heads of state were the two consuls, Rome's most senior magistrates. Their power was less than a king's power because they balanced each other and ruled for only one year. The Greek thinker Pylorus, writing in the second century BCE, praised the Roman constitution. He thought monarchy, aristocracy, and democracy were all flawed, but he argued that the system of consuls, Senate, and comitia contained the best of each type of state.

As Sulla made his way home, he was followed by a young man. The boy mocked and jeered at Sulla the whole way, knowing that it was now much safer to do so. Sulla patiently ignored him until he reached his door. Here he turned and said to the youth, "You should not mock me, because you will prevent anyone in future laying down such power as I have." These words have been taken as a prophecy of Caesar's reign, for Caesar never laid down his dictatorship. He lost it when his assassins took his life.

CHAPTER 2

THE ROAD TO POWER

During the troubled times of Caesar's teenage years, even his tender years and inexperience were no guarantee of his personal safety. Caesar was closely tied to Sulla's enemies, through his aunt Julia's marriage to Gaius Marius. Marius appointed Caesar *flamen dialis*, a priest of the Roman father-king of the deities, Jupiter. Cinna, coruler with Marius, arranged to marry his daughter Cornelia to Caesar. These developments almost certainly put Caesar on Sulla's list of adversaries. Things came to a head when Sulla had finally returned to Rome permanently from war. He demanded that Caesar divorce Cornelia. The young man refused. Instead, he went into hiding, becoming a fugitive.

After some hair-raising escapes, Caesar made his way to Asia Minor, modern-day Turkey. At one

This bust shows Julius Caesar as a boy. The future leader of Rome was born into a turbulent time in Roman history.

point, he had to bribe one of Sulla's patrol commanders with two talents (132 pounds, or 60 kilograms) of silver to let him go. Sulla showed his customary shrewd judgment of character. When he gave in to the arguments of his advisers that Caesar was a mere boy and ought to be spared, Sulla still exclaimed:

> Very well then, you win! But mark my words, the man you want me to spare will one day destroy the party which you and I have defended for so long. There are many Mariuses in this man Caesar.

The political party that Sulla said Caesar would destroy was the Optimate Party. Sulla was right, as usual. Caesar would follow in the footsteps of his uncle Marius and drive his opposition from power.

CAESAR RISES THROUGH THE RANKS

Caesar escaped to the East and joined up with the Roman army there. War had broken out again with Mithradates, and it was in these years that young Caesar had the adventures described earlier. He won his civic crown in 80 BCE at the siege of Mytilene and fell in with the pirates on his way to Rhodes in 75 BCE. Returning to Rome in his late twenties, Caesar found it gripped by yet another crisis: the slave revolt of Spartacus. A force of around one hundred thousand escaped slaves had formed an army and roamed across Italy for several years, causing considerable alarm. They were eventually defeated by Marcus Crassus in 71 BCE. Caesar was elected to his first post on the cursus honorum in 72 BCE, that of military tribune, and in this junior office he probably served in the campaign against Spartacus.

In 69 BCE, Caesar was appointed to the next rank, that of quaestor. He was to assist the Roman governor of Spain. But before he could go out to the province, he had a solemn duty to perform. He had to attend the funeral of his aunt Julia. This was to be no ordinary funeral, since Julia had been the widow of none other than Gaius Marius. Caesar showed his political colors as one of the Populares by having a statue of Marius carried in the procession. No one had dared to show images of this people's hero since before Sulla's reign. And in his funeral oration, Caesar made it quite clear how important he thought he and his family were:

> My aunt's mother was a descendant of kings, namely the Marcii Reges . . . and her father, like all the Julii, was descended from gods—Venus in fact. Thus her stock can claim both the sanctity of kings, who reign supreme among mortals, and the reverence due to gods, whom even kings must obey.

Afterward, Caesar went to Spain, where he got his first real experience of administration in the provinces. The historian Suetonius tells a most interesting story about Caesar's time in Spain. It is said that, while in the Temple of Hercules at Cadiz, Caesar came across a statue of Alexander the Great. Reflecting upon Alexander's career, the thirty-one-year-old Caesar shed a tear, bitterly complaining, "At an age when Alexander had already conquered the whole world, I myself have achieved nothing at all memorable." Apparently, he left the province immediately and sought greater honors at Rome.

ROMAN POLITICS : OPTIMATES AND POPULARES

With a very few exceptions, every Roman politician belonged to one of two main political parties, the Optimates and the Populares. These were not as well organized as the political parties of today. They more or less resembled factions, the members of which were united by shared views and goals.

The Populares, which means "the men of the people," represented the masses. They did this not because they necessarily liked the common people but because they knew that with popular support they could become very powerful leaders. They therefore supported policies like the distribution of state-owned land to ordinary citizens. They were generally reformers, like the Gracchus brothers, Gaius Marius, and Caesar himself.

Opposed to them were the Optimates, which means literally "the best men." They aimed to preserve conditions in which the senators together could dominate the common people. Thus they tended to be conservative, that is, opposed to reform. They did not like farmland to be distributed because many senators possessed and managed huge estates at very low rent. Sulla was an Optimate, and so was Pompey after him.

Caesar now took horrible risks in his attempt to gain power. When the high priest (*pontifex maximus*) died, Caesar stood for election to the post. He borrowed huge sums to bribe the voters, and he told his mother on polling day, "Today you will see me either become high priest or an exile."

In 65 BCE, Caesar took his next step in the cursus honorum. He became *aedile*, again thanks to bribery. As aedile, he continued to run up his debts, putting on shows of unheard-of splendor. These included plays, public feasts, processions, and single combats between 320 pairs of gladiators. This made Caesar extremely popular with the masses, and at the height of his popularity he had the old statues of Marius and the trophies of his victories gilded and set up again at the capitol, from which Sulla had removed them. The large faction of Marius, which had been dejected and leaderless without him, now began to see Caesar as their savior.

Caesar became praetor in 62 BCE, and shortly afterward he went out to govern the province of Spain, where he fought a war against the native people. This war gave him his first experience of being a commander in chief, and the captured booty allowed him to patch up his shattered finances. He returned to Rome with only the highest office yet to win: the consulship.

A VAST AND GROWING EMPIRE

Caesar served in Spain during both his quaestorship and praetorship, but Spain was just one of many Roman provinces. In Caesar's lifetime, most of the lands surrounding the Mediterranean had been conquered, and by the time he died, this conquest was almost entirely completed. The Mediterranean Sea was the heart of the Roman Empire, so much so that in Latin it was known simply as Mare Nostrum (Our Sea). Undisputed control of its shipping lanes meant that transport of people and goods was cheap, speedy, and relatively safe—at least by ancient standards. But this had not been achieved easily.

The northern border of Italy, as the Romans thought of it, was the Po River, not the Alps, as it is today. The conquest of Italy was completed in 272 BCE with the capture of the city of Tarentum. Looking outward, Rome next came into conflict with the North African city of Carthage, and from

264 BCE to 146 BCE, they struggled between them for mastery of the western Mediterranean. In the course of these so-called Punic Wars, the Carthaginian general Hannibal ravaged Italy, but Rome eventually prevailed. As a result of its Punic victories, Rome gained control of Sicily in 241 BCE, Spain and much of Greece in 197 BCE, and the provinces of Africa (modern Tunisia) and Achaea (southern

By the time of Caesar, Rome had conquered a vast territory. Here is an engraved municipal charter for a Roman colony in Spain, circa the first century BCE.

Greece) in 146 BCE. The Romans moved into Asia Minor (modern Turkey) in 133 BCE and Pontus in 63 BCE. Cyrene became a province in 75 BCE, Crete in 66 BCE, and Cyprus in 58 BCE.

The colonization of Cisalpine Gaul, the area between the Po and the Alps, began in 218 BCE, but by 50 BCE its inhabitants were still not Roman citizens. As will be seen later, Caesar fought for them to have this privilege, and they supported him loyally. Rome conquered Transalpine Gaul, a small area in the south of modern France, by 129 BCE. It was from here that Caesar was to mount his Gallic War, afterward claiming to have conquered all the Gauls and to have extended the province to the Rhine and the Atlantic.

A THREE-WAY ALLIANCE

When Caesar returned to Rome in 60 BCE, he overcame opposition to his election to the consulship with the help of two powerful men, with whom he now formed the famous threeway alliance known as the triumvirate, literally, "the rule of three men." One of Caesar's most important financial backers had been Marcus Crassus.

Not all people within Rome's empire were content. Shown here in gladiatorial combat is Spartacus, who would lead a slave rebellion, the Third Servile War, in 73 BCE.

Roman general Crassus, shown here absorbed in his papers, was one of the players involved in the struggle to determine who would lead Rome.

Crassus was the richest man in Rome. He was a competent general—he had served under Sulla and had defeated Spartacus—but he did not have the military brilliance of Caesar. Nevertheless, his wealth made him an extremely valuable ally because bribing the electorate was so important.

The other figure who was bound to dominate the political scene at this time was Gnaeus Pompeius, known as Pompey the Great since his defeat of the last of Marius's forces in Africa in 81 BCE. He had saved Rome from the menace of pirates in the Mediterranean, and he had finished off the troublesome Mithradates of Pontus once and for all. He had returned to Rome early

POMPEY

There have been few careers as phenomenal as that of Pompey. He was just twenty-three years old when he raised an army of fifteen thousand men, on his own initiative, to join forces with Sulla in 83 BCE. After several overseas missions to destroy the last of Sulla's enemies, Pompey held a triumph in Rome at the age of twenty-five. It was unheard of for a man to stage a triumph when not yet a senator, but Sulla allowed it. In 77 BCE, at the age of twenty-nine, Pompey was sent to quell a rebellion in Spain with the powers of a consul, and at the age of thirty-six he was made consul. Such youth in the highest office of Rome was, again, unheard of.

By 67 BCE, the problem of piracy throughout the Mediterranean had become so serious that the food supply of Rome itself was threatened. Pompey was appointed to a three-year command (yet again, unheard of) against the pirates. He was granted the power to assemble ships and recruit 120,000 legionaries and 5,000 cavalry. He was to have twenty-four senators as his legates (deputies) and absolute authority throughout the Mediterranean and 50 miles (80 km) inland. Pompey defeated the pirates and ended the threat from King Mithradates VI of Pontus before returning to Italy and disbanding his forces.

After his military successes, he passed the decade

This marble bust of Pompey the Great now resides in the Ny Carlesberg Glyptotek art museum in Copenhagen, Denmark.

of 60 to 50 BCE quietly enough in Rome, basking in his former glory. His later struggle with Caesar for power seems to have been half-hearted. His actions seem as if they were prompted more by his senatorial advisers than his own desires. Perhaps it was because of these conflicting influences that he was, in the end, to be so fatally indecisive.

in 61 BCE, and although he disbanded his army, he could still count on the loyalty of his veterans if a political crisis should develop into civil war. Crassus, Pompey, and Caesar came together in 60 BCE because together they had enough power to defeat any opposition from the rest of the senators. Crassus had huge amounts of money and considerable influence with the merchants of the Roman middle class. Pompey had an unchallengeable military reputation and the loyalty of the army. Caesar had overwhelming influence with the common people and, most important, the political skill to bring his two colleagues together.

The triumvirs got most of what they wanted. Pompey had a portion of state land handed over to his veterans for farms, and the peace settlements he had made in the East were ratified by the Senate. Crassus could look forward to being given a major military command in the coming years, and he secured tax cuts for himself and his business friends. Caesar received the consulship, the highest office, in 59 BCE. But the Senate, whose job it was to allocate provinces to the magistrates, gave Caesar a province within Italy. Since Italy was now at peace, he would have no chance for further military glory. His opponents in the Senate could count this as a success.

Although Caesar's consulship was relatively uneventful, at the end of the year fortune intervened in his favor. Metellus Celer, who had been nominated for governor of Transalpine Gaul in 58 BCE, suddenly died. Caesar persuaded the Senate that in addition to Cisalpine Gaul and Illyricum, which he had already been given, he should receive Transalpine Gaul to govern for five years. It was in Gaul that he was to make his name as a great commander.

CHAPTER 3

CONQUERING GAUL

A popular myth still persists about the Roman era and the Gauls, the Roman Empire's neighbors to the north across the mighty Alps mountain range that divided Italy from northern Europe. Beyond this natural, protective border, there was a chaotic, lawless land of uncultured barbarians, constantly at war with each other and with their more civilized neighbors. Many Romans imagined this to be true, at least. Modern popular narratives of the barbarian hordes opposing the powerful but civilized Romans continue even today. The Romans looked down upon and sometimes outright despised the Celtic and Germanic peoples that inhabited these northern lands, considering them primitive and dangerous.

Many of these prejudices were the natural result of the longtime conflict between the

The Pont Du Gard aqueduct that spans the Gardon River in southern France is one of the more famous relics of Roman engineering remaining in Europe.

Romans and these peoples. The Gauls, who ruled much of modern-day France, even sacked Rome in 396 BCE, a stinging defeat the Romans still felt wounded by. But the Romans were the aggressors as often as the Gauls and others were. Their military expansion into an empire that spanned a continent was proof enough.

Nor were the Gauls entirely primitive. There were sixty or so independent groups in Gaul as Caesar found it. Although in remote areas, some of them were organized as tribes and others had powerful kingships. Still others had annually elected leaders and senates, much like the Romans. Their major settlements were the *oppida*, hilltop sites fortified with massive ditches that also functioned as towns. The oppida were also administrative and commercial centers where coins were minted and craftsmen had their workshops. Caesar's allies, the Aedui, were one such well-organized people.

CONFRONTING THE HELVETII

Caesar took up the rule of his provinces in 58 BCE. Almost right away, the opportunity for a military expedition presented itself. The Helvetii, who lived just beyond the frontier, intended to migrate to western Gaul, and their quickest route was through Roman territory.

Caesar refused to allow this, probably quite rightly. The Helvetii numbered around 150,000 (Caesar's account claims 376,000), a quarter of whom were fighting men, whereas Caesar had just one legion present. He demolished the bridge at Geneva and fortified the riverbank, using the one legion he had with him. This would give him time while his other three legions arrived from Italy. He also gave orders that two new legions be recruited there.

When they learned that Caesar had barred their way, the Helvetii took a route that avoided Roman territory but that skirted its northern border. This route took them through the lands of the Aedui, Rome's oldest allies in Gaul. When the Aedui complained of the devastation the Helvetii were causing, Caesar had an excuse to act. Although governors were forbidden by law from taking their armies outside their province, the law included a clause that allowed them "to defend the state interest," even if this meant marching over the border. That was all the opportunity Caesar needed.

With his six legions and their auxiliaries, about sixty thousand men altogether, Caesar followed the Helvetii into central Gaul. He harassed them, but he was not strong enough to mount an all-out attack. After some weeks, he broke off contact to attend to the army's food supply. The Helvetii understood this as a sign of weakness and followed him.

ROME'S MILITARY MIGHT

The Roman army was the largest force to be trained and organized for warfare before modern times. This organization meant that the instant Caesar arrived in Gaul, he could issue orders that his men could understand and carry out. Similarly, troops arriving from different parts of the empire could easily work alongside each other and know exactly what to expect of their comrades.

The largest Roman unit was the legion, a force of around five thousand men. It did not have a permanent commander. For a specific operation, a legion or group of legions could be placed under the command of a legate, a brigadier-general in modern terms. The men were trained as heavy infantry to kill their enemy at close quarters with javelins and swords. Most men also had secondary roles as specialist engineers of one kind or another. Still others served as clerks or surveyors. The legion consisted of ten cohorts.

A cohort was a unit of about five hundred men. One or more cohorts could be grouped under the command of a military tribune, a colonel in modern terms. At all other times, the senior centurion would be in charge. The cohort was made up of six centuries.

The century was a unit of about eighty men. It was commanded by a centurion, who had an *optio*, a second in command, to assist him or take over if he was killed. Centurions rose from the ranks, and in modern terms were more like sergeant-majors than company commanders. The century was further divided into ten sections of eight men. Each section, called a *contubernia*, shared a leather tent, a mule, a hand-mill for making flour, a cauldron for cooking, and various other pieces of equipment.

Now the Romans had the chance to fight a defensive battle on ground of their own choosing. Caesar took up a strong position on a nearby hill and after a hard battle defeated the Gauls. When they fled, leaving behind their supply wagons, Caesar knew he had won. He threatened to attack any nearby tribe who gave the Helvetii food. After a few days, hunger forced them to surrender.

After dealing with the Helvetii, Caesar moved on toward the Rhine to defeat another enemy of the Aedui, the Germanic leader Ariovistus. Caesar drove Ariovistus and his men out of Gaul. Caesar then put his army into winter quarters in the lands of the Sequani. It was almost impossible to campaign in the winter in Gaul. It was very cold, and there was not enough forage for the army's pack animals to eat. The men also needed to rest.

DIVIDE AND CONQUER

The campaigns against the Helvetii and Ariovistus were typical of Caesar's strategy in Gaul. By treating some Gallic peoples (like the Aedui) as friends, he greatly increased his ability to dominate the region. By gaining Gallic food supplies, he could take his army on longer expeditions. With the use of their soldiers, particularly their excellent cavalry, he increased his striking power. And because the Gauls were always at war with each other, he could always get involved in fighting, on the grounds that he was helping Roman allies.

In the spring of 57 BCE, Caesar recruited another two legions. He now had four that the Senate had given him and four raised at his own expense. With this force, he set off deeper still into Gaul, where, he claimed, a group of peoples known as the Belgae were "hatching a plot against the Roman people." Caesar made an alliance with the Remi, a local tribe. The rest of the Belgae, who according to Caesar had an army of over three hundred thousand men, set out to attack Caesar and the Remi. Meanwhile, Caesar asked his friends, the Aedui, to plunder the farmland of the Belgae. In the end, the sheer size of their huge army proved disadvantageous to the Belgae. They quickly ran out of food supplies and, with the attack on their farms, were forced to return home. Once their enormous force had split up, Caesar was easily able to attack the communities of the Belgae one or two at a time. Some surrendered their towns to him; others he defeated in battle.

The year 56 BCE was given over to smaller operations. Caesar sent legions to different parts of Gaul to deal with peoples not yet conquered. He himself attacked the Veneti, who lived on the Atlantic coast. These people were mariners and plied the trade routes to Britain, so to defeat them Caesar had to become the first Roman to command a fleet on the ocean. Defeat them he did, and he dealt harshly with them. Caesar executed their council of elders and enslaved the rest of the population. In his account of the war, he says he did so because they had behaved treacherously. But, like any Roman commander, Caesar would have made a lot of money from the sale of the slaves, and this may have been a more important reason.

In 55 BCE, Caesar felt that the situation in Gaul was calm. He now made two amazing crossings to the lands beyond. First, he built a bridge across the

This illustration depicts Julius Caesar leading a battle during the Roman invasion of Britain in 55 BCE, an incursion into uncharted new territory for Rome at the time.

wide, fast-flowing Rhine. This was so his army could punish the Germanic tribes on the far side, who had been raiding Gaul. This had never been done before, and neither had his next achievement. He took a force of two legions to Britain, an almost unknown island at that time. But he could not stay there for the winter. With the weather getting worse, Caesar soon sailed back to Gaul.

In 54 BCE, setting out earlier in the year, with his ships and plans improved by the experience of the previous year, Caesar invaded Britain again. This time he had five legions and two thousand cavalry. He marched inland as far as the River Thames (in London), and several British kings surrendered to him. However, since he returned to Gaul without leaving behind a garrison, it does not seem that Britain was in any sense conquered.

ROME'S TACTICAL STRENGTHS

The battle Caesar fought with the Helvetii is a good illustration of the superb flexibility of the Roman army in battle. The troops were thoroughly drilled so they could move into different formations almost automatically, which most barbarian armies could not do. Much of the legion's flexibility came from its division into ten cohorts. The cohorts could be deployed in a variety of ways. One very effective deployment was the so-called triple order of battle. The ten cohorts were arranged in three lines, one behind another.

The three-line battle formation had a number of advantages. First of all, if the battle was long, the second line could move forward through the first and take over the fighting, with fresh men and more javelins. Of course, the enemy could also push fresh troops forward, but because they did not have an organized drill for doing so, this could be a chaotic moment. Tired and wounded enemy soldiers moving to the rear might spark off a panic, causing the whole army to turn and run. The Roman system helped the legionaries to overcome their natural human fears.

If an enemy force unexpectedly appeared to the Romans' flank or rear, the third line could turn to face it. This was very reassuring for the first and second lines facing the enemy in front. Caesar describes this happening in the battle with the Helvetii, when their allies, the Boii, suddenly appeared on the Roman right.

When there was a lull in the fighting, the first line could stay alert and drawn up for battle while the cohorts of the second and third lines would start to entrench and build a camp. If the enemy attacked, the resistance of the first line would allow time for the second and third lines to stop digging and get ready to fight. Once the camp was finished, the first line would march inside the entrenchments.

REBELLION IN GAUL

It appears that Caesar was called back to Gaul by the worsening situation there. As it turned out, he had some very serious fighting ahead of him. The legions' camps for the winter of 54–53 BCE had to be spread far apart. This was because a poor harvest

ROME'S MILITARY ENGINEERS

It is no exaggeration to say that Roman legions made war with the spade just as much as with the sword. At Alesia, the legionaries' skill in fabricating all manner of fortifications from local materials was important to the victory. Both on the march and in the face of the enemy, it was the Roman army's amazing feats of engineering that made it one of the most successful the world has seen.

There was no obstacle they could not cross. In 55 BCE, Caesar built a bridge across the mighty Rhine, near modern Koblenz. Here, the fast-flowing river is 1,200 feet (365 m) wide and up to 25 feet (7.6 m) deep. Yet in ten days, using local timber and the saws, axes, and ropes each squad carried, Caesar's men were on the far bank. To top this achievement, they then built a fleet of transport ships that carried them to Britain in the late summer.

Caesar's men often had to assault formidable fortresses, like the hill towns of Gaul or the Greek city of Massilia. Here, again, their engineering skills were decisive. They built high towers from which to fire arrows, lances, and rocks onto the defenders on the walls. While missiles from the Roman towers kept the enemy's men under cover and prevented them from firing back, the legionaries constructed an earth ramp up to the level of the enemy battlements. Leather-covered screens and galleries were also used to protect the soldiers as they worked. Once the ramp was completed, the Roman troops could rush over the walls and defeat the enemy at close quarters.

Roman engineering helped the empire dominate its enemies militarily. Here, Roman soldiers man a catapult, one of their most effective siege weapons.

and food shortages meant that several tribes had to share the burden of feeding the garrisons. The Gauls suddenly rebelled, and it was easy, at first, for them to overcome the isolated Roman forces. The Eburones massacred fifteen cohorts (7,500 men) near their camp at Atuatuca. The Roman army had to work hard to restore its rule in Gaul. But even when it did, the peace was short-lived.

In 52 BCE, almost all of Gaul united against the Romans under one leader: Vercingetorix. Even Caesar's allies, the Aedui, turned on him. Vercingetorix had learned the tactical lessons of earlier campaigns. He refused to mass a big army of infantry for a pitched battle. He realized that the Gallic infantry had rarely done well in such large formations, and large numbers of men were difficult to feed. Instead, he decided to wage a fast-moving guerrilla war in which the Gauls could use their cavalry to their advantage. According to the plan, the Gauls destroyed their own supplies whenever the Roman army was near.

In order to get food, the Roman foragers were forced to go further afield in smaller groups. Then the Gallic cavalry could pick off the isolated Roman units.

Although Vercingetorix's tactics had some success, Caesar captured the towns of several communities and punished them severely. Eventually, Caesar tracked the Gallic leader to Alesia, where he had based his main force. Alesia was an oppidum (a fortified hill town), too strong for the Romans to assault. Both sides had problems, and the scene was set for a mighty siege. In the town, the Gauls had enough food for thirty days. By rationing it, they might last until a large army collected from the rest of Gaul could rescue them. If they managed to hold out, Caesar would find himself besieged by the Gallic relief force!

Caesar's solution was to build a bigger system of field fortifications than any Roman general before him. He set his seventy thousand men to work, surrounding the town with 11 miles (17 km) of fences, ditches, booby traps, watchtowers, and camps. Around this, he built another similar 14-mile-long (22-km) fortification, this time facing outward, to protect his men from the Gallic relief force.

By the time the relief force arrived outside Alesia, Vercingetorix and his men were agonizingly hungry and had been considering cannibalism. Nevertheless, they still fought hard to harass the

This modern replica of fortifications Caesar built to defeat the Gallic tribes in the siege of Alesia (modern-day Alise-Sainte-Reine, France) offers a glimpse of Roman warcraft.

Romans as the relief force tried to break through. This phase of the battle alone lasted four days and took place over an area 5 or 6 miles (8–9 km) across. Caesar's account says there were more than two hundred thousand Gauls in the relief force. This is probably an exaggeration, but it was certainly a desperate struggle. Both sides seemed to know that this was a fight to the finish.

The fall of Alesia and the capture of Vercingetorix put an end to widespread resistance in Gaul. After two more fairly peaceful years in the

Vercingetorix, Gallic chieftain of the Arverni tribe, is shown laying down his arms in surrender to Julius Caesar after the Roman military victory. He was later executed.

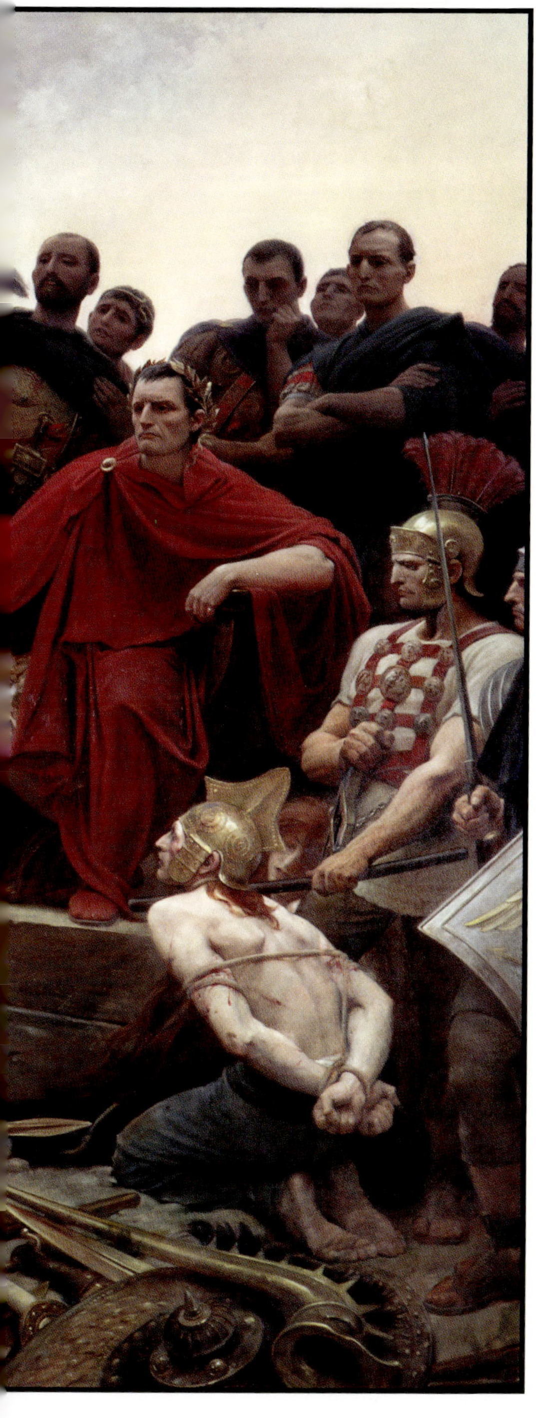

province, it was time for Caesar to step down from his command. He was fifty years old. He had gained a great reputation in Gaul, a large and loyal army, and great wealth. But the turbulent world of Roman politics called to him. The scene was set for Caesar's next great challenge: the war with Pompey.

CHAPTER 4

CAESAR'S CIVIL WAR

Despite his hands being more or less full with military campaigns in Gaul, Caesar did not neglect affairs back home. A secret meeting with Pompey in Cisalpine Gaul in 56 BCE yielded a plan for the triumvirate to advance its interests. Crassus and Pompey would become consuls in 55 BCE and then pass a law extending Caesar's command of Gaul through 50 BCE. Crassus would be given a military command on an eastern front against the Parthian Empire (then rulers of modern-day Iran) in hopes that he could score a major victory against one of Rome's then most formidable rivals. But these carefully laid plans backfired when Crassus was defeated and wiped out with much of his force in Mesopotamia, near the town of Carrhae, in modern-day Turkey. Rome's richest man had been outmaneuvered, and it had proved a fatal mistake. Historians debate whether or not Crassus held the balance between Caesar and Pompey. Some claim the latter two would have come into conflict eventually no matter what. Regardless, the remaining two members of this once stable triumvirate began to drift apart.

A civil war between Caesar and Pompey broke out at the end of 50 BCE, when Caesar refused to disband his forces at the end of his term of office in Gaul. He feared that as a powerless private citizen, his numerous enemies in Rome simply might kill him. On January 10, 49 BCE, he led his troops across the Rubicon River, which marked the end of his province and the start of Italian territory. Here, at the point of no return, he uttered the famous line, "*Alea iacta est*" ("The die has been cast").

Caesar, with only a few troops, rapidly overran Italy. Pompey could not mobilize his forces quickly enough, and Caesar reached many of the areas where they were gathering in time to win the troops over to his own side. Pompey therefore left Italy to Caesar and headed for Greece, his old campaigning ground, taking the Senate with him.

Caesar handed over Rome to the praetor Lepidus and the Italian garrisons to Marcus Antonius (Mark

Julius Caesar crossing the Rubicon River in 49 BCE is one of the enduring symbolic images of his eventual conquest of Rome.

Antony), while he himself headed for Spain, where the Roman commanders were loyal to Pompey.

At the beginning of the civil war, Pompey declared that all who were not with him were against him. Caesar, on the other hand, stated that he would consider all who were not actively against him as if they were on his side. By adopting this less rigid approach, Caesar opened up a path to forgiveness for waverers, and in the end he pardoned most of Pompey's defeated supporters.

Caesar's diplomatic skills proved to be a decisive advantage. Both he and Pompey were generals with the military skill to destroy their enemies in battles and sieges. Pompey may even have been a more skilled general than Caesar in this respect. But Caesar, with his diplomacy, could turn enemies and potential enemies into useful friends and allies. This did not just remove threats but turned their strength to his own advantage.

THE TRIUMPH OF CAESAR

En route for Spain, Caesar left his subordinate, Junius Brutus, with three legions to besiege Massilia (modern Marseilles), which was still an independent Greek city at this time and had allied with Pompey. Caesar continued on with six more legions to fight a swift campaign against the Pompeian generals Afranius and Petreius. Not wanting to spill the blood of fellow Romans unnecessarily, Caesar managed to

This French historical print depicts Caesar's forces waging their siege and naval assault on Massilia (later known as Marseille, France) during his civil war.

outmaneuver his enemies and cut them off from all food supplies, thus forcing them to surrender. It was a brilliant operation and one that could only have been achieved with the veteran army Caesar had forged in Gaul.

Caesar now controlled the whole of the western Roman Empire, and, picking up Junius Brutus and marching back to Italy, he turned his attention to Pompey himself. Pompey was dug in at Dyrrhachium (modern Durres, in Albania) and protected by very strong naval forces. To avoid the enemy's warships, Caesar sneaked his force across the Adriatic and landed unopposed 100 miles (160 km) south of Dyrrhachium on January 5, 48 BCE. He marched up the coast to engage his opponent but

was severely defeated on the battlefield. Caesar later commented that if Pompey had had the energy to follow up his success, he could have won the campaign then and there. Instead, Caesar was permitted to fall back in good enough order to Pharsalus, in Thessaly.

At Pharsalus, Caesar offered battle, and Pompey drew up his forces to accept. This was clearly to be a very decisive battle. When the armies were arrayed and ready to advance, both commanders are said to have shuddered. It was clear that by the day's end one of them would be the champion of the world, while the other would be the most wretched man in it. And to decide this issue, thousands of their brave countrymen were about to give their lives. The wretched man turned out to be Pompey. With fifteen thousand of his men killed, he fled for Egypt, where he was murdered as he stepped ashore.

In hot pursuit, Caesar arrived in Alexandria with three thousand legionaries in the late summer. He learned of Pompey's

Italian artist Paolo Uccello's painting *The Triumph of Julius Caesar* shows Caesar's triumph over Pompey in the Battle of Pharsalus in 48 BCE, another step in his march to victory.

death but soon found himself caught up in the Egyptians' own civil war. He had brought only a small force and was besieged until March 47 BCE. It was during this winter that Caesar had an affair with Cleopatra. Soon after, she had a child, whom she named Caesarion (Little Caesar). While Caesar was entangled with intrigues in Egypt, revolt had flared anew in Spain and Africa. Pompey's son, Pompey the Younger, was there, continuing the fight. But Caesar's priority was to return to Italy and spend three months arranging matters in Rome, which Mark Antony had managed badly.

On New Year's Day, 46 BCE, Caesar landed in Africa again to deal with those of Pompey's forces who had survived the attack on Pompey. This was to be no easy campaign. He had

Caesar further cemented his power in 49 BCE. This illustration shows his forces at the time of the Battle of Ilerda (near modern Lérida, Spain).

A BOLD AND NATURAL LEADER

In Gaul and throughout the civil war, Caesar called upon his men to face great dangers. They hardly ever flinched. Why? Caesar understood that, as well as knowledge and expertise, the key to leadership was to be self-sacrificing and to set a personal example. One night, on a journey through Gaul, Caesar and his officers were driven by a storm to take cover in a forester's hut. Inside, there was a bed in a tiny room that would contain only one person. "Places of honor must be given up to the strong," he said, "but we should give the necessities of survival to those most in need." With these words, he ordered Oppius, an officer who was weak with illness, to take the bed. Caesar and his other companions lay down outside the door and took what shelter they could.

Caesar's willingness to share danger with his troops also inspired them. He called them comrades, which was unusual for an upper-class general. Before the battle with the Helvetii, a tribe from what is modern-day Switzerland, he sent away his own and his officers' horses. This was so his soldiers could be sure he was not planning to run away, which in turn made them feel he was confident of victory.

The troops also loved Caesar because of his generosity toward them. Normally, legionaries were charged for their rations, and this could cost them up to a third of their pay. In Gaul, Caesar stopped ration charges, allowing the men to keep more of their money. He insisted only on strict discipline on the battlefield. "My soldiers fight just as well when they are stinking of perfume," he is said to have boasted, words that many Romans would have found shockingly unmilitary.

given his veteran forces their longed-for discharge, so he was forced to fight with raw and untried troops. Against him were not only the desperate remnants of the Pompeian faction but also the local Numidians. The arrival of Caesar's main force was delayed until April, but then he took immediately to the offensive. The result was an uncontrolled and chaotic battle at Thapsus. Here, despite Caesar's endeavors, many Romans were butchered, though Caesar won the battle.

The rebel leaders and some of their troops escaped and moved the resistance to Spain. It was here that the civil war was brought to a close. At Munda, on March 17, 45 BCE, Julius Caesar had his last victory. Like Thapsus, it was a merciless, blood-drenched slaughter. The mass of corpses is said to have

surrounded the town like a wall.

But afterward, there was peace within the empire at last, although outside it the Parthians were

Legionnaires march on a Roman-built road. The well-trained and battle-tested soldiers Caesar deployed were a decisive factor that allowed his military genius to prevail.

still considered to be a threat. None now challenged Caesar's power. In Rome, they waited to see what he would do with it.

CHAPTER 5

THE DICTATOR AND HIS DOWNFALL

Coming home for the winter season of 45–44 BCE, Caesar returned in triumph. He worked on some political reforms that had long eluded him and began planning a new military campaign against the Parthians. Part of his platform now became reconciliation, rather than vengeance. This meant pardoning former enemies, including some of Pompey's followers who had survived the civil war. They would now be allowed to return from exile. Statues of Sulla and Pompey were re-erected. These maneuvers were partly out of genuine respect and partly to appease those who might be bitter in defeat or feel humiliated by it.

In addition to these diplomatic gestures of honor, Caesar did not hesitate to pile honors upon himself and accepted any and all from all sides. His friends even proposed new honors. Shrewdly, so did his enemies. The latter reasoned that inflating Caesar and raising him upon a pedestal would actually turn off many Roman citizens.

Unfortunately, Caesar could not resist such overtures to his vanity. He was made a god before the public, with a statue bearing the legend *Divus Julius* ("the god Julius") put up in his honor. As presumptuous as these actions were, the Senate could have overlooked this. Even later Roman emperors, such as Augustus, were formally considered gods. But their main gripe with Caesar was the trappings of leadership he took up. He sat in a golden chair during Senate meetings and donned the purple robes and high red boots worn long ago by Roman kings. When others hailed him as a king, he corrected them, swearing off this honorific. In reality, Caesar was dictator for life of Rome in all but name.

POLITICAL, SOCIAL, AND OTHER REFORMS

Once Caesar had won undisputed mastery of the Roman state, he was able to solve some of its many problems.

Caesar also carried out a number of major

THE JULIAN CALENDAR

One serious issue that may seem, upon the surface, to be insignifcant was that of the Roman calendar. Although Earth takes roughly 365 days to orbit the sun, before Caesar the Roman year had only 355 days. March, May, July, and October had thirty-one days, February had twenty-eight, and all the others had only twenty-nine days. This meant that the calendar year tended to get ahead of the solar year. To stop this from happening, the priests would decide, when they thought it necessary, to add an extra month after February, which happened roughly every two years. Unfortunately, this was done so badly that by 47 BCE the middle of winter was occurring as late as the middle of March. Caesar decreed that 46 BCE would have 445 days, to set things straight, and every year after would have 365 days. An extra day would be added every fourth year. With a slight adjustment by Pope Gregory XIII in 1582 CE, this is the system of years and leap years we still use today.

social reforms. He had to disband and resettle the enormous armies of the civil wars. To do this, Caesar undertook a program of colonization, establishing new towns in nearly every part of the Mediterranean. Each community received a few thousand settlers, along with their families, and each colonist was granted, free, his own share of farmland. Not only soldiers, but about 80,000 of the poorest people in the city of Rome were settled by Caesar in this way.

These colonists played an important role in spreading the Roman way of life, as the new towns they founded gave people in the provinces a demonstration of its advantages.

By moving the unemployed out of Rome, Caesar helped to restore law and stability in the capital. The huge mass of these people, who relied for sustenance on the free distribution of corn, had been a volatile political element for nearly a century. Under these new measures, the recipients of the corn dole were reduced from 320,000 to 150,000. Caesar also ruled that the larger estates had to recruit at least one-third of their labor force from the free population. Previously, the almost total use of slaves was putting citizens out of work. Caesar also wanted to increase the population. Therefore, he provided rewards for the fathers of large families. He also turned his attention to the upper classes. He tried to improve their morals by passing so-called sumptuary laws that put limits on the wearing of luxurious costumes or jewelry and on the eating of too much exotic food. The historian Suetonius said that Caesar's patrolmen

Corinth, Greece, is shown here, with Roman chariots entering. Caesar founded a new city there in 44 BCE, which became the Greek provincial capital of the Romans.

sometimes entered houses and removed forbidden dishes from the tables after they had already been served!

Caesar's political reforms had important implications, too. He increased the Senate to nine hundred members and took the opportunity to reward his followers by including them in the enlarged body. More important, a law was enacted that limited an ex-consul's period as a provincial governor to two years. Caesar was determined that no potential rebel would have a long time abroad to build up a power base of money and troops. This is what he himself had done in Gaul, and what Pompey had done in the East. This law was therefore an important contribution to the empire's future stability.

FIGHTING THE PARTHIANS

With Rome's domestic affairs in order, Caesar planned a war against the Parthians. Caesar's former colleague and sponsor, Crassus, had lost both his life and his army to them back in 53 BCE. Caesar was not about to leave this score unsettled. The Parthians were an Iranian people who had led a nomadic life on the fringes of the civilized world until 247 BCE. In this year, according to tradition, they invaded Mesopotamia, conquered the inhabitants, and proceeded to rule over them for nearly five centuries. The Parthians made their capital at Ctesiphon-upon-Tigris, about 20 miles (32 km) southeast of modern Baghdad.

At the height of their power, the Parthians ruled lands from modern Syria to Pakistan, and whenever Rome attacked them, they proved themselves dangerous enemies. Parthia's plains lent themselves to the use of cavalry, and the Parthians made sure that theirs could outmatch the Romans. They employed both heavily armored cataphracts, who fought at close quarters with lances, and lightly armored mounted archers who could discharge their weapons, then escape at a gallop, still firing.

Classic Parthian tactics were for the archers to wear down the enemy with countless arrows. Then the cataphracts charged in and finished the job.

When Caesar was assassinated, he was about to set out for the East with an army. What would have happened if he had survived to fight the Parthians? Perhaps he would have failed like Crassus and forever ruined his military reputation. Or perhaps he could have extended the Roman Empire to the borders of India. In 116 CE, a century and a half after Caesar's death, the emperor Trajan did indeed capture Ctesiphon and even penetrated as far as the Persian Gulf. However, Parthia proved impossible to hold and was soon abandoned.

THE PLOT AGAINST CAESAR

With Caesar's departure for the Parthian war imminent, more than sixty conspirators banded together to assassinate Caesar while they had the chance. They were led by Gaius Cassius and Marcus and Decimus Brutus. Many of the dictator's Gallic War officers and former friends had also joined the conspiracy. Rather than do away with Caesar secretly in some quiet spot, they decided that he should be

This marble bust is of Marcus Brutus Junius the Younger. Brutus joined the conspiracy against Caesar, even though he had become part of his inner circle.

killed at a public meeting of the Senate. This was to be a clearly political act, they reasoned, more of a public execution than a murder. And when the deed was done, they decided to show proudly their bloodstained hands, rather than flee, as a sign that they were Rome's liberators. On March 15, the Senate was to meet in the Theater of Pompey, and this was agreed as the time and place for the fatal act.

Ancient authors recorded that numerous signs forewarned Caesar of his death. The soothsayer Spurrina told him that his life would be at risk and that the danger would come no later than the Ides of March (March 15). Word came to Rome that a herd of horses that Caesar had made sacred were shedding tears. In the city itself, a bird known as the kingbird was torn to shreds by a flock of other birds. Some say that Caesar even foresaw his death and accepted it. On his last evening alive, he dined at Lepidus's house, along with Decimus Brutus. When the conversation turned to which sort of death was best, Caesar's preference was for one that was "swift and unexpected." And indeed, he refused any sort of bodyguard, entrusting himself to the protection of the senators. During his last night, Caesar dreamed that he was soaring above the clouds and meeting the god Jupiter, while his wife was distressed to dream of Caesar's body streaming with blood. But he was not discouraged, and on the morning of the fifteenth, Caesar left home for the Theater of Pompey.

When he arrived at the theater, he saw Spurrina and mocked him: "The Ides have come," he said. "Yes they have come," replied the soothsayer, "but they have not yet gone." As Caesar was going into the theater, a well-wisher put into his hand a letter giving him details of the conspiracy.

However, the dictator was pressed for time, and the document was found later, unread. One of the plotters kept Mark Antony, who was Caesar's loyal deputy and a man of great physical strength, talking outside.

Inside, as Caesar took his golden seat, the conspirators gathered round, as if to pay their respects. One, Tillius Cimber, seized hold of him, while another, Casca, struck the first blow, which glanced off, slightly below the throat. At first Caesar whirled round to defend himself, but as the assassins fell

This detail from the famous 1789 painting by Vincenzo Cumuccini, *The Death of Caesar*, shows the dictator being assassinated in 44 BCE.

on him he gave in, drawing his toga over his head and legs, so as to fall decently covered. Some say he died without a word. Others say that, as Marcus Brutus struck the second blow, Caesar said in disappointment, "You too, my child?" The assassins plunged their daggers, leaving twenty-three wounds in Caesar's body, and in the struggle several conspirators wounded themselves. The dictator slumped down at the base of a large statue of Pompey, spattering it with blood. Those few onlookers who did not flee immediately could not avoid the

impression that Pompey, Caesar's greatest foe, had presided over the whole affair.

Following a period of rioting and confusion

Mark Antony gave a speech over the body of the fallen Caesar during a public funeral. His emotional speech prompted many of Caesar's angry followers to riot.

in Rome, civil war broke out anew between Caesar's supporters and his assassins. Lepidus and Mark Antony joined forces with Octavian, Caesar's nephew and heir. They defeated Marcus Brutus and Cassius at Philippi, not far from Pharsalus, in 42 BCE and ruled together as a second triumvirate until 37 BCE, when Lepidus was pushed aside. Afterward, Octavian and Antony quarreled and raised armies against each other. Octavian emerged victorious after the naval battle of Actium in 31 BCE. Octavian, who took the name Augustus Caesar, then ruled alone for forty-four years, completing Julius Caesar's work of turning the empire into a monarchy and becoming Rome's first and greatest emperor.

The first century BCE was a revolutionary epoch for Rome. At its beginning, the Romans called their state a republic, although in reality it was an oligarchy ruled by the senatorial families. Under the republic, Rome had massively expanded its empire.

However, by the time of Jesus's birth, the situation was very different. Augustus was securely established as the monarch and sole ruler of the Roman Empire, and although many republican traditions were preserved, they had become formalities. And the empire stopped expanding its territory. This change, the so-called Roman Revolution, was the most dramatic in the empire's history, and it is why the study of Roman history is subdivided into the republican period, which covers all the time before Augustus, and the principate, which spans from Augustus to the fall of Rome.

Augustus avoided the office of dictator, which had proved disastrous for Caesar. Instead he styled himself as princeps, or chief. Augustus was also called imperator, or general. From this Latin word is derived the modern English word "emperor."

As commanders in chief, the emperors made sure that none of their subordinate commanders had large enough armies to become a threat. This taming of military power was, naturally enough, very important in ending Rome's territorial growth. The consuls and other magistrates continued to be elected every year, but half of them were now elected only with the emperor's recommendation.

Caesar had won this right in the last months of his rule. The ancient power of the veto held by the tribunes of the people over the Senate was now assumed by the emperors, and this was an important power indeed.

Caesar was the central actor in the Roman Revolution. Sulla, whose dictatorship foreshadowed Caesar, used his rule to shore up the oligarchy. In this he was swimming against the tide of history. Caesar recognized that the empire had grown so large that unless it was brought firmly under one man's control, its various parts would continuously fight each other. Many hundreds of thousands of lives were lost in the wars he fought. Perhaps, if he had chosen not to act, other wars would have occurred with even more death and destruction.

This statue of Caesar in Rome, Italy, is one of many relics of his reign. While his ambition undid him, he is still remembered as a leader, politician, general, and legend.

HOW DO WE KNOW?

All of the events described in this book took place more than two thousand years ago. How is it possible that they are still known? The answer is that written records based on eyewitness accounts were made at the time, and these, amazingly, have survived the centuries. The original documents, of course, perished long ago, but before they did, copies were made, and these copies were in turn copied. It is worth remembering that before printing became widespread at the end of the Middle Ages, copying by hand was the only way books could be made. The oldest surviving copy of the history that Caesar wrote, *On the Gallic War*, was made by monks in the ninth century CE. Of course, we also know of some accounts that existed in ancient times but have since been entirely lost.

It is useful to divide the accounts of Caesar's times into two groups. One group, written by contemporaries of Caesar's, is important because the writers had access to the most accurate testimony. The other group of sources, written later on, but still in ancient times, is also very useful today because the historians who wrote them had access to accounts from those contemporaries that have since been lost, and so are unavailable to us.

Of the contemporary accounts, all in Latin, the most important are the commentaries of Caesar himself. These include the commentaries *On the Gallic War* and *On the Civil War*. Caesar witnessed almost all of the events he describes, but that does not necessarily make them true accounts. They were as much propaganda as history, and when reading them one needs to be wary of Caesar's attempt to glorify himself and undermine his opponents.

Oppius, who published *Life of Caesar*, and Balbus, whose *Diaries* must have included useful details, were both officers who served under Caesar. Sadly, both of their accounts are lost, as are the *Histories of Asinius Pollio*, which dealt with the period from 60 to 42 BCE. Livy, who lived from 59 BCE to 17 CE, wrote a near-contemporary account. Although much of his history of Rome from the founding of the city survives, the section dealing with Caesar is lost.

The only later writer to use Latin was Suetonius, born around 70 CE. His account *Divus Julius* (*The God Julius*) includes many scandalous personal details, which make it an entertaining read, if not a very accurate one. The rest of the later writers wrote works in Greek, which all survive.

Plutarch (50 CE to 120 CE) wrote paired biographies of the great Greeks and Romans called the *Parallel Lives*. He paired Caesar with Alexander the Great. Appian of Alexandria (born around 95 CE) and Dio Cassius (born around 164 CE) wrote about Caesar's times as part of much larger projects. There also exist some very brief Latin summaries of Livy's lost account. These were made some time after 400 CE and are thought to be rather inaccurate.

censor A Roman magistrate; two were appointed every fifth year and were in charge of taking the census and reviewing senators' qualifications.

consul The highest Roman magistrate, two of which were appointed annually and commanded the main armies..

curule aedile A Roman magistrate that ranked between the quaestor and the praetor; two were selected each year to look after the city's business.

deification The process by which a mortal becomes a god.

democracy A political system in which power is ideally shared by all citizens.

dictator In Rome, an emergency rank under which, in a very serious crisis, one man was given supreme power (above even the consuls) for six months.

forage Green or dry vegetation cut to be fed to animals in addition to their grain ration.

magistrate A government official appointed to perform certain military or civil tasks.

monarchy A political system in which power is held by one person.

oration A formal speech given on a ceremonial occasion.

praetor A Roman magistrate appointed to serve in Rome for one year and then sent out to govern provinces for two to three years as a propraetor.

propaganda Information, usually inaccurate or biased, that is publicized to achieve certain political goals by influencing public opinion.

quaestor A Roman magistrate that served as a deputy to a provincial governor, assisting him with finances and food supplies.

American Classical League
860 NW Washington Boulevard, Suite A
Hamilton, OH 45013
(513) 529-7741
Website: https://www.aclclassics.org
The American Classical League was founded in 1919 for the purpose of fostering the study of classical languages in the United States and Canada.

The American Institute for Roman Culture
1101 West 34th Street, Suite 730-174
Austin, TX 78705
(512) 772-1844
Website: http://romanculture.org
The American Institute for Roman Culture works to preserve and protect Rome's extraordinary and unique cultural legacy through education, outreach, and action.

Classical Association of New England
Department of Classical Studies
Wellesley College
106 Central Street
Wellesley, MA 02481
Website: http://caneweb.org
The Classical Association of New England is the professional organization for classicists in New England. Its mission is to foster the study of the

classical world through the associations many activities and resources.

Department of Greek and Roman Studies
University of Victoria
3800 Finnerty Road
Victoria BC V8P 5C2
Canada
http://www.uvic.ca/humanities/greekroman
The University of Victoria's Department of Greek and Roman Studies offers a wide-ranging, multidisciplinary program combining the study of language, literature, history, and archaeology centered on the ancient Mediterranean world.

Society for the Promotion of Roman Studies
Dr. Fiona Haarer, Roman Society
Senate House, Room 252, South Block
Malet Street
London WC1E 7HU
England
Website: http://www.romansociety.org
The Roman Society is the leading British organization dedicated to the study of Rome and the Roman Empire, including its history, archaeology, literature, and art. It has a broadly based membership, drawn from over forty countries and from all ages and walks of life.

WEBSITES

Due to the changing nature of internet links, Rosen Publishing has developed an online list of websites related to the subject of this book. This site is updated regularly. Please use this link to access this list:

http://www.rosenlinks.com/LANW/caesar

Bancroft Hunt, Norman. *Living in Ancient Rome*. New York, NY: Chelsea House, 2009.

Batstone, William W., and Cynthia Damon. *Caesar's Civil War* (Oxford Approaches to Classical Literature). New York, NY: Oxford University Press, 2006.

Boardman, J., J. Griffin, and O. Murray. *The Oxford Illustrated History of the Roman World*. New York, NY: Oxford University Press, 1988.

Caesar, Julius, and Carolyn Hammond, trans. *The Gallic War: Seven Commentaries on the Gallic War with an Eighth Commentary by Aulus Hirtius* (Oxford World's Classics). New York, NY: Oxford University Press, 2008.

Connolly, Peter. *Greece and Rome at War*. Mechanicsburg, PA: Stackpole Books, 1981.

Markel, Rita J. *The Fall of the Roman Empire* (Pivotal Moments in History). Brookfield, CT: Twenty-First Century Books, 2007.

Nardo, Don. *The Fall of the Roman Empire*. New York, NY: Lucent, 2001.

Ogilvie, R. M. *The Romans and Their Gods*. London, UK: Pimlico, 2000.

Scarre, Chris. *The Penguin Historical Atlas of Ancient Rome*. New York, NY: Penguin, 1995.

Steele, Philip. *The Roman Empire*. New York, NY: Rosen Publishing, 2009.

Strauss, Barry. *The Death of Caesar: The Story of History's Most Famous Assassination*. New York, NY: Simon & Schuster, 2016.

Southern, Pat. *Julius Caesar*. Charleston, SC: Arcadia, 2001.

Wilcox, Peter. *Rome's Enemies: Gallic and British Celts*. London, UK: Osprey, 1985.

Appian of Alexandria. *The Civil Wars*. New York, NY: Penguin, 1996.

Baker, Rosalie F., and Charles F. Baker. *Ancient Romans*. New York, NY: Oxford University Press, 1998.

Boardman, J., J. Griffin, and O. Murray. *The Oxford Illustrated History of the Roman World*. New York, NY: Oxford University Press, 1988.

Caesar, Gaius Julius. *The Civil Wars*. Cambridge, MA: Harvard University Press, 1914.

Caesar, Gaius Julius. *The Gallic War*. Cambridge, MA: Harvard University Press, 1917.

Claridge, Amanda. *Rome: An Oxford Archaeological Guide to Rome*. New York, NY: Oxford University Press, 1998.

Fuller, John Frederick Charles. *Julius Caesar: Man, Soldier, and Tyrant*. London, UK: Eyre & Spottiswoode, 1965.

Gelzer, Matthias. *Caesar: Politician and Statesman*. Oxford, UK: Basil Blackwell, 1969.

Hornblower, Simon, and Anthony Spawforth, eds. *The Oxford Classical Dictionary*, 3rd ed. New York, NY: Oxford University Press, 1996.

Nardo, Don. *The Fall of the Roman Empire*. New York, NY: Lucent, 2001.

Plutarch. *Lives*. New York, NY: E. P. Dutton & Co., 1910.

Powell, Anton, and Kathryn Welch, eds. *Julius Caesar as Artful Reporter: The War Commentaries as*

Political Instrument. London, UK: Duckworth, 1998.

Rice Holmes, Thomas. *Caesar's Conquest of Gaul*, 2nd ed. Oxford, UK: Clarendon Press, 1911.

Rich, John, and Graham Shipley, eds. *War and Society in the Roman World*. New York, NY: Routledge, 1993.

Stevenson, Tom. *Julius Caesar and the Transformation of the Roman Republic*. New York, NY: Routledge, 2014.

Suetonius Tranquillus, Gaius. *The Twelve Caesars*. New York, NY: Penguin, 1957.

ABOUT THE AUTHORS

Margaux Baum is an editor and author from Queens, New York.

James Thorne graduated from University College, London, in 1995 with a B.A. in archaeology. He then served in the Royal Tank Regiment, undertaking operational tours of Northern Ireland, and as a United Nations peacekeeper. In 2000, he graduated with distinction from the master's program in ancient history at the University of Manchester, England. He continues to live in Manchester, teaching and undertaking research on Caesar's Gallic campaigns.

PHOTO CREDITS

Cover, pp. 3 Leemage/Universal Images Group/Getty Images; cover (background), p. 19 Heritage Images/Hulton Fine Art Collection/Getty Images; pp. 7, 16, 60–61, 68–69 Print Collector/Hulton Archive/Getty Images; p. 21, 28 DEA/A. Dagli Orti/De Agostini/Getty Images; p. 25 Culture Club/Hulton Archive/Getty Images; p. 35 De Agostini Picture Library/A. Dagli Orti/ Bridgeman Images; p. 37 Universal Images Group/Getty Images; pp. 38–39, 52–53 Hulton Archive/Getty Images; p. 41 PHAS/Universal Images Group/ Getty Images; p. 45 Sean Russell/Getty Images; pp. 56–57 © Mary Evans Picture Library/Alamy Stock Photo; pp. 62–63 Getty Images; p. 66, 76–77, 82–83 Private Collection/© Look and Learn/Bridgeman Images; pp. 70–71 Musee des Arts Decoratifs, Paris, France/ Bridgeman Images; pp. 72–73 © Prisma Archivo /Alamy Stock Photo; p. 86 Museo Nazionale del Bargello, Florence, Italy/Bridgeman Images; 88–89 Leemage/Hulton Fine Art Collection/Getty Images pp. 90–91 Archive Photos/Getty Images; pp. 94–95 © Vito Arcomano/Alamy Stock Photo; interior pages background images © iStockphoto.com/kikkalek5050 (sky), Triff/Shutterstock.com (map)

Designer: Brian Garvey; Editor: Philip Wolny; Photo Researcher: Philip Wolny